TAKE ADVANTAGE OF YOUR CRISIS

Christian Lee Vaughan

Take Advantage of Your Crisis

Published by Spines

ISBN: 979-8-89383-221-1

TAKE ADVANTAGE OF YOUR CRISIS

ACHIEVING GROWTH AND RESILIENCE: EMBRACING OPPORTUNITIES IN TIMES OF CRISIS

CHRISTIAN LEE VAUGHAN

CONTENTS

INTRODUCTION

Explore a path to empowerment through 'Taking Advantage of Your Crisis.' When faced with stagnation and despair, I can assist in changing your outlook and uncovering the silver lining in EVERY circumstance. Allow me to lead you towards a more optimistic emotional state and demonstrate that a crisis signifies the start, not the end. Reclaim your beautiful life and rediscover hope once more.

Successful individuals are those who are truthful with themselves. They choose to refrain from blaming others for their challenges and instead take immediate action!

"The dance of life is bound by what you really want and your fears," said Tony Robinson.

Having hope is contagious. Hope is the most important building block of a flourishing life and is the pathway to REAL fulfillment and happiness.

"Hope is one of the 24 universal character strengths, and it is within the virtue category of transcendence. It is about expecting something positive, being future-minded. You may also notice this strength in someone who shifts the focus in a conversation towards a silver lining."

"Hope is one of two character strengths most strongly linked with happiness," an article from Ball State University, *VIA Character Strength Spotlight: Hope.*

Anyone in a crisis feels hopeless. It's a natural response. I was in that place for a long, long time until I started taking advantage of my problems.

Once you've internalized that you're truly not alone in this battle of life, then I can give you the tools to be able to take your life back, get your relationships filled back up with love, and experience peace, tranquility, serenity, and calmness like never before. Come step with us on the good side of humanity. It's so much more fun!

CHAPTER 1
WHAT EXACTLY IS THIS BOOK ABOUT?

Discover how to reignite passion in your life with 'Taking Advantage of Your Crisis,' a program that transformed my life and can do the same for you. Learn three unique tools to overcome any challenge. It's time to experience positive changes in every area of your life.

I promise you will become completely hooked on this program!

At the bare minimum, try the program for seven days. Take 1-2 hours out of your day and focus. I mean, come on, how many weeks have you already lived? All those weeks with nothing done. Just sitting there wondering why nothing is happening to you. How bad could it be to try something for seven days? Nothing else has worked, right? If you don't like this after seven days, go ahead and try something else.

You won't need to go elsewhere, though. I'll give you the tools right here. The cold, hard facts. A book you can always come back to if you need the juice back in your life. Let's lace up those shoes and start today!

Personally, when I started the program, I went in for 30 days. After 30 days of complete focus, I didn't stop. I found myself wanting more. I kept the momentum, and it became my everyday routine. I had to build new habits, or nothing was going to change.

All YOU have to do is three simple things starting today:

1. Be honest with yourself.
2. Follow the guidelines with no exceptions.
3. Complete focus on gratitude (think about the people you love and who love you) or (start thinking about the positive in every situation around you).

For this to work, you must have a positive mindset as soon as possible. Positivity and gratitude are the building blocks that will guarantee lasting change. I will teach you how to create a positive emotional headspace with only a few simple tricks.

I promise it won't be overly complicated. There is zero reason to make this complicated. I know the feeling of wanting to keep it simple. Trust me, I am all about taking the path of least resistance.

I wanted to start feeling good again, though! Don't you? That's why I designed this. I wanted to know the facts and start making things happen now! I made this program to better myself. There was no way I was going back to my old life.

I dove right into my research like a madman. I was determined. I spent weeks investigating hundreds of theories on how to be truly happy. I started to notice a pattern of events in these theories about finding happiness. I honed in on that pattern.

I only researched concepts that provided proven results. There was no way I was going through a ton of work for no outcome. I've done that enough. I needed to know that if I were to work this hard at something, I had to have a guarantee.

This book contains no nonsense. I'm not promoting products. I won't deceive you. If I can overcome my challenges, I believe you can too. This has ignited a long-desired feeling within me. Let's begin to alleviate the suffering in your crisis. We need to acknowledge our emotions, address them truthfully, and then we can begin to feel the results.

Nevertheless, when we find ourselves trapped in a negative mindset, we often need help. Our view of the world becomes skewed, making it difficult to alter our current beliefs.

You have the choice to be in a positive head space or a negative head space. This power is inside you.

You cannot keep covering up your emotions and expecting them to change. That is a law of the universe.

There are many laws in the universe. When something is a law, it'll never change. This law will never ever change, no matter what you try to do to resist it. These laws must be followed, or Mother Nature will take its course on you. I define the law of the universe as "without immediate action, such as personal growth or physical motion, you will get rigid or die."

Regaining a positive emotional state can reignite passion and vitality in your life. I can guide you on how to achieve this, but you must look past the distractions and focus on reality. These techniques will empower you to navigate life's challenges. While difficulties may still arise, these tools can help diminish problems that once seemed insurmountable, leading you to experience serenity and see issues in your life fade away.

Don't ever forget, everyone has problems. Problems can either be good or bad. You just need to decide what type of problem you want in your life. Don't ever expect there to be no problems. This is the downfall of many.

You must be okay with failing. You have to change your focus to see that when you fail in life, it gives you a chance to grow. Without failure, we would never grow into the person we were meant to be. Failure sculps our personalities. Growth is usually painful, too, but it is vital for life to exist. This is a law of the universe.

Keep in mind, once you've learned these tools, this knowledge doesn't leave you. In life, you will get overwhelmed. You will find that you're not experiencing joy in everyday life, and overall, you will find that your life is stressful again. Don't worry; just come back to these tools. They are right there in your mind, or if it's been too long, just restart the book.

We all deserve to be who we truly are. These tools will launch you into a different dimension of human existence. The dimension we were meant to be in. A place of growth. A place of love and compassion. A destination you can only experience once you're honest with yourself and force yourself to change your perceptions and beliefs. We need you back in a positive emotional headspace.

It is time to start Taking Advantage of Your Crisis!

CHAPTER 2
POWER OF THE PROGRAM: PHILANTHROPY CAME TO ME

After entering the next dimension of human existence, exclusively through the process of 'Taking advantage of your crisis,' I have manifested an intense, overwhelming, burning desire to help humanity. Before this process, there had been zero contemplation in my life about helping a complete stranger. Let alone writing this book. This, yet again, proves that this process works.

I started to discover that I was now possessed of the traits of a humanitarian. The desire to be charitable, humane, idealistic, kind, and public-spirited completely engulfed me.

I absolutely love the feeling I get when I cheer someone up or surprise them with some sort of compassion. I know how painful things can be. I know how life can seem like a total task. My perspective was so out of wack that I had to completely change the way I looked at the world. I was in a crisis. Between being who I was "supposed" to be and who I "thought" I wanted to be.

I'll admit I was really caught off guard when these charitable feelings washed over me. All I was doing was following some program. A program I had designed for myself.

I started using self-discipline to stay in a positive emotional state. I define self-discipline as; "the battle between the voice of our human instincts and the voice of our hearts.

I finally saw that, within us, everyone holds the ability to be good or to be evil. I like to call them the light and the dark. We decide if we turn on the lights or if we stay in the dark. This will determine the quality of your life. It's up to you. However, if you're not honest with yourself, it just won't work.

So, first, be honest with yourself, and then get into a positive emotional state. Lastly, start moving your body. This will create emotion. Motion creates emotion. If you feel emotionally stuck, MOVE!

CHAPTER 3
MY EARLY YEARS: ANALYZING ITS IMPACT ON MY ENTIRE LIFE

I grew up in a commercial fishing family. Located in a very small town on an island in Southeast Alaska. I always used to say we really weren't any different from other people in America. We run machinery (boats) over water (instead of land) to harvest food. We are ocean farmers.

I was raised with three other brothers and one sister. I fall right in the middle of them. I am the middle child. Yes, I know the term "black sheep". Oh, how words can define you.

We were a really hard-working family. I began hard physical labor at age 11, along with my two older brothers. Of course, I didn't know any better at the time. I thought my dad was the most powerful person in the world. If he said to start working, well, then I just did. We didn't stop unless he told us to.

My dad was a very strong-willed man. An Alaskan fisherman. Built to withstand anything the ocean can throw at him. You can tell he has been through a few "life dances" just by looking at his old, salty face.

I have yet, to this day, met a man who works as hard as my dad. That man has some serious passion and drive, maybe not directed in the correct way. Nevertheless, he is a role model for pushing on. A role model for pushing against the resistance of social hypnosis, at least with his career that is. Is this the definition of a real man?

Fresh out of high school, my dad hitchhiked his way from Detroit, Michigan, to Alaska in 1982. Yes, hitchhiking across the country was legal back then.

When I was about 12 years old, I remember asking my dad why he would ever think about moving to Alaska. Most people don't like the places they grow up in.

I understand that, but I hated growing up in Craig, Alaska. Population: 800 people. Stuck on an island. With nowhere to go. Everyone was your family. This brought intense anxiety into my young life. The result was a bad habit of isolating myself.

In return, my dad told me this: "I grew up watching my dad work at car dealerships and laundry mats, and he even took school photos. I just knew that type of life was not for me. Something was telling me to do more."

9

I never met my grandpa on my dad's side, but it sounds like he was just as tenacious as my dad.

My father's biggest point was this: he decided a long time ago that he would never end up like his dad. Not just the fact of ending up like his dad, but the passion went even further into my dad's soul. He decided one day to take massive action to change the outcome of his life.

Now, I am not going to sit here and try to say I know the dynamic between my dad and his dad. All I know is that my dad decided one day to make a change. Something so radical that everyone in his life thought he was going crazy. He laced up his shoes. He quit lying to himself about his situation and took massive action. The outcome of my dad's life could easily have been much different.

We all have the power to control some part of our destiny. Don't just sit around and wait for it to happen! You can flow with the river, but you have to at least steer the canoe in the right direction.

Amongst having a solid work ethic, my dad was very emotionally abusive towards me. He would yell frequently at all of us, including my mom. I always felt so bad for my mom.

He would justify his yelling by using the excuse that

he had to endure so much pain and anxiety (fear) that everything should be perfectly in line when he arrived home from fishing. When there was any sort of disruption in the pattern of his life, he would exterminate the issue immediately.

Early on, he started to notice that people responded quickly, with no hesitation, when he yelled. He discovered how to use fear to get what he needed. His bad emotions continuously were rewarded time and time again. This only amplified the intensity of his yelling.

Nowadays, he still lives in that emotional state of fear. My dad let his fears control his life. Made it all the way, only to be alone. People can't stand to be around him. His fear-based approach to life is going to spiral him into a massive crisis.

Then what is life all about? How can we succeed in our work while everything else crumbles? I put in my work, right?

Now, my dad has a limited family life; no one wants to work for him, and he's beginning to isolate himself. Everyone is scared of him. He's never heard the truth in his life. He lies to himself about his fears, and people lie to him out of fear. Insane that a person can live an entire life like this. It takes an enormous amount of willpower and/or alcohol.

Even though I never want to say my mom played a

part in my crisis, she definitely did. A lot of her "motherly actions" monumentally changed me for the worse. These events really added to my crisis.

My mom grew up in Alaska. She was born and raised in Southeast Alaska. While she was growing up, they would move from logging camp to logging camp as the years went by. Going wherever new land was opened up to harvest lumber. This resulted in a sheltered life for my mom and her siblings. They grew up solely with their immediate family, living in an Alaskan logging camp in the middle of nowhere for years!

My mom's parents were devoted Christians. Seventh-Day Adventist. The Sabbath on Saturday was never missed. The last of an old school bread of people who were once at the mercy of Mother Nature.

My grandpa, not biological, was another one of those Alaskan men who decided a long time ago to put his head down and work hard.

I can't imagine what they went through back in the old days of pioneering the logging industry in Southeast Alaska. Life was much harder, physically, anyway.

All my mom ever wanted in life was a family. It seemed as if that was her only goal. She wanted kids and as many as she could get.

So, you can imagine what it was like when my dad came swooping in from Michigan. A knight in shining armor. To take my mom away from her dysfunctional, sheltered, logging family.

I believe it was my dad's first taste of narcissism. He was overwhelmed with the feeling that he could have power over people's lives with what he said. Nothing physical ever, but he could destroy your soul with words alone.

I always loved my mom. She was a loving, devoted mother. It was her primary job, her entire life. So, I hope I feel like my mom was there for me.

In our family, it seemed normal that my mom would take care of us until we were old enough to go out and work on the boat with my dad.

However, when it came to me, the middle child, my mom, for some reason, didn't want to let me go. She fought my dad like crazy. She did not want me to start working. She was deathly afraid of her children growing up, especially me.

I don't know what's going on in her personal life journey. However, what I do know is this: my mom sheltered me from a very young age. She became dependent on me for her happiness. She wouldn't let me experience pain on my own. She was a helicopter mom. Always there to make sure I would never feel any pain. This seemed noble, but it backfired intensely on her.

Ultimately, I had come to a crisis in my life where I

felt too attached to my mom. I could not use my own wings to fly. I couldn't use my own words. I couldn't think outside the box. The box that she had created in my mind.

This was incredibly hard for me to see. I see now that her fears controlled her life, just like my dad. Her fear consumed her and, ultimately, everyone in her life. I have no idea how she deals with my dad's anger, still to this day, right up in her face for 35 years straight. That man doesn't show signs of backing down, either. I pray for both of them. That one day, their fears can be lifted. That they can find humility and become honest with themselves and each other.

Honesty is the only way to true happiness. This is the law of the universe. I would rather choose to be honest, wouldn't you? Honesty is simple. Honesty will save you from an incredible amount of unnecessary problems in the future. Try it!

CHAPTER 4

MISCONCEPTIONS ABOUT WHAT IT MEANS "TO BE A MAN": MEN NEED TO START EXPRESSING THEIR EMOTIONS.

When I was growing up, all the men in my life told me to work hard and shut up. Alaska is a brutal place to work. You get what you deserve. Keep your head down and work hard because life is a bitch.

These men are spiritually sick. They have let fear control their lives. They are worn out. They use words like, "Well, this is what it's like being a man" to cover up their broken hearts.

There are many stigmas out there, but this one I'd like to get rid of. Men DO NOT have to dull their emotions to be "strong"!

In society today, men are required to deny their feelings. Not given a chance to feel it and heal it.

These overwhelming feelings are demanded in order to cover up emotions while simultaneously conforming to what people have created with the phrase "to be a man." This stigma is destroying the souls of men. This fear-based approach to becoming a man is destroying everyone in the realm of their existence.

Men must start to realize the law of the universe says, "Men and women both carry the weight of immense emotion." Men must be able to use all their emotions.

Guys, I need you to start crying. I need you to start being emotional for the right reasons.

The men in this country need time to heal. Don't you want them to be the "man you thought they were"?

I believe the people in this world who own up to who they truly are are the strongest by far. These people use their traits to an advantage.

Man or woman. Make a change for the positive, even if it's a major change in your life. Be authentic and let your true colors shine.

To be able to express your pain and cry is human nature at its most simple level. These emotions are required for emotional growth. You must feel it to be able to heal it. This is a law of the universe.

When I was a teenager, I saw older fishermen as role models. As we have learned, these men are spiritually broken, full of fear, unhappy, depressed, anxious, angry, etc.

Will the outcome of their choices reflect the emotional state they are in? Yes, it will. The outcome will not be good. Not good for anyone in the realm of their existence.

Naturally, early on, these "role models" had pushed their views onto me. Their style of life coaching was all they knew. I know their intentions were based on love, but the results were not love.

Once I took a step back and looked at my life honestly, it was clear to me that role models in my life were unconsciously destroying my soul.

I didn't realize that over time, I was slowly changing my perspective, conforming to what I thought my life should be from my role models' life blueprints. I never focused on what I needed for my happiness.

I make sure to stay away from any negative emotional thoughts. The thoughts that were implanted in my brain from spiritually broken men. I came to the conclusion that these uncharted traits of fear were something that I had to live with. I quickly realized that it was not okay to let them take over my mind, though. I continue to force myself to stay focused on the positive. We have the power to choose what emotional state we are in. It's just hard to do at first, but then it becomes a habit. The advantage in every situation will eventually present itself naturally to you.

How can an old, salty Alaskan fisherman ever do anything positive with his life when he lacks an ounce of positivity, humility, gratitude, willingness, or honesty? He can't. This goes for all people, men and women, who are miserable inside and hard-shelled on the outside. You are not fooling anyone. You are doing more harm than good in this situation.

This may be an extreme and/or rare view of the modern, physically labored man, but it was all I knew. It was my entire world. Nothing else existed in this world. I was transformed into one of those broken men who raised me. No matter what I felt, I had to be like them, or literally, it would be the end of the world as I saw it. These men clearly worked way harder than me; I knew deep down that I could not be accepted into this world. They saw me as a failure. A waste of their time. I tried to keep up for a long time. I really did. I realized that deep down, I downright did not enjoy commercial fishing. It became mundane and stressful.

I kept thinking I'd rather be dead if I were to let them down. To be a failure in their eyes was a complete disappointment to me. I was afraid. I was afraid deep down that they wouldn't love me or respect me as a person.

In that moment of time, life really seemed to be

over. Everything was done out of fear. Everyone was in an emotional state of fear, so the outcome was fear.

I never thought I could live up to their expectations. I just knew I didn't have the personality to build a fishing career for myself.

Out on the ocean, at any moment, life can get extremely stressful. It's a daily roller coaster of emotions. A constant state of survival.

I know that early on in life, the emotional state I was in was fear. We all react to fear in a distinct way when we are children. My reaction as a child was to do everything exactly right. I turned into a people pleaser.

I thought if I could please everyone, there wouldn't be a reason to get yelled at. I didn't have to feel worthless again if I just made people happy. As long as I did a little extra work and kept my mouth shut, they could never get mad at me. This created havoc in every part of my life.

CHAPTER 5

IT'S ASTONISHING HOW WE ARE INFLUENCED AS CHILDREN: HUMAN INSTINCT VS. LISTENING TO OUR HEART

"Our "fight or flight" reaction may be our best-known expression of our survival instinct. This response set is triggered when we (all animals) perceive a situation as a threat to our existence; our sympathetic nervous system makes rapid emotional, psychological, and physical changes. Emotionally, we feel either fear or anger intensely.

When you were a child, what type of survival instinct did you have? Fight or flight? "Fawn or freeze?"

Source from Jim Taylor Ph.D., book: The Power of Prime, titled 'Is Our Survival Instinct Failing Us? Year: June 12, 2012.

My mom never did anything to get away from my dad. He is a professional manipulator. He mentally owns her. I believe in narcissism. That's my personal guess, anyway.

Since my mom was sheltered and beaten during childhood, it confirmed to my dad that he really could have controlled her with no consequences. His extreme anger was always rewarded in the end.

Once your brain begins to associate certain behaviors with rewards, you'll eventually develop a craving for the behavior, even when you don't realize it. This is a law of the universe.

I mention this about my parents, these inherited behaviors because they directly affected my life to the point of fantasizing about suicide. I was in complete hopelessness. I was in a constant state of anxiety and fear. I never stopped chasing anxiety. In the end, I wanted the anxiety to stop. It was driving me insane. I constantly felt like I had never fully accomplished a task. I felt as if I would never be enough. I was forced to go with the flow and become a people pleaser. This was not a conscious decision. This was a decision made in a crisis. A decision made out of fear is based on a negative emotional state. This choice was made to meet the expectations of others. It prevented me from introspection. I was unable to discern my true purpose. I had no purpose. I never got a chance to weigh out the options for my strengths and weaknesses. I never had the chance to really look at myself and say, "This is your life." I was constantly trying to do the "right" thing for other people.

Today, I do not care what my original family and friends think of me. I don't let it bother me one bit. Now, I make decisions based on what my heart is telling me and the cold, hard facts of life. I understand that I can't play God in my life, but I do know we have the power to change our destiny. We do have a choice in some aspects of life. We

need to tap into our inner selves, get rid of our fears, listen to our hearts, and take massive action.

There's an entire community out there right now, living in their idea of a fulfilled lifestyle. They are truly happy. This isn't happiness from getting quick cash or a new car. This is serenity, where we do not live in fear.

You need to be okay with who you are as a person. Shed your fears, and you'll blossom like a flower. Stop looking for happiness in things around you.

You must look within your soul to discover true happiness.

CHAPTER 6

TAKE ACTION: IF YOU'RE EMOTIONALLY STUCK, MOVE!

I am the one who took tremendous action after a crisis in my life. Nobody was going to do it for me. That is a law of the universe. I made a change in my life, for me and for the better of humanity. I didn't put my head in the sand and expect the world to conform to me.

That is what I used to always do when things got uncomfortable, unbearable, and downright tough. Clearly, the path of least resistance sounds better, especially when you're in a bad emotional space. I tried that option more than once. Ignoring the problem always multiplies the intensity of the problem.

For once in my life, I decided, at that moment, to be honest with myself, which led me to take gigantic action in my life. To stop expecting new results from old habits. If I truly wanted to see new results in my life, I knew there was no other option but to form new habits.

No doubt, I wanted all the amazing things in life, too. A new car, a house, a family, a normal life... It seemed as if life wasn't on my side and a "normal" life wasn't in the cards for me.

However, I finally realized that no matter what happens in life, I had to start pushing back. I started pushing against this resistance that natural forces on us. I forced myself to build self-discipline. I started building different perspectives on negative events. I started looking at the advantages in each situation.

Why do I have to be so passionate about it? I tried every option I could to have life stop or at least slow down. I thought I deserved one day off from this life thing, right?

The thought of working every day to wake up and do it again completely took over me. The thought of being a slave to the almighty dollar consumed me. Slowly but surely, the emotional space I created spiraled me into a crisis. I was hypnotized.

Quite frankly, this put me in a position where change was demanded. Crisis demands change. The time to contemplate is over. To me, my only options were to get lost in the dead zone (social hypnosis) of life or die.

I couldn't handle the thought of giving up spiritually or conforming to the hypnosis of society. This colli-sion of life events revealed my true personality. I now could see my path. I knew deep down what needed to be done.

Then, I was able to make a decision in the right direction to promote spiritual growth within myself. I finally felt what it was like to have options of my own. I stopped worrying about what everyone thought. I began to live a life worth living. A life that aligned with who I thought I was and where in this world I would be most useful.

When I started to become useful in society, it sparked a feeling in me. A feeling thought only to come from objects around us. This started the process of designing my own life.

CHAPTER 7

DISCOVERING MY INDIVIDUAL JOURNEY: IF I ACHIEVED IT, YOU CAN TOO!

I chose to focus on the advantages of the situation I was currently in. I switched my focus to the positive in every situation. When a negative emotion wandered into my mind, I instantly started my favorite incantation. I would start repeating over and over to myself, "every day in every way, I am getting stronger and stronger."

Try it; it really works. Find an incantation that works for you and start using it.

I decided to do incantations for 30 days straight. I was literally brainwashing myself to think positively. This allowed me to automatically focus my energy on the advantage of the situation.

I started taking advantage of the problems in life, seeing the good in all the bad, and most of my fears disappeared. This brought me peace. A feeling that was very unfamiliar but welcome.

All of a sudden, my mind started working again. The path was clear. I thought back to a time in my life when I was really motivated, happy, and full of passion. It came to me that I was in a positive and creative headspace. I didn't care about the outcome of the situation. I didn't care what people thought of me. I was confident and focused. Visualizing what I wanted for my end goal the entire time. This made me work hard on the task at hand.

However, when I began to fail in my projects continually, I slowly created a negative headspace for myself. Unconsciously, everything around me turned negative.

The law of the universe says, "Focus equals reality." No matter what the situation, there is always an advantage. Control your emotions. Think positive and create a gratitude list. Your outlook on life will slowly change. You will have a new perspective.

I decided to give this gratitude thing an honest try. I became hooked as soon as I started. The feeling that comes from harnessing the power of gratitude is addicting. This unconsciously began to alter my perspective on the world as I knew it.

After years and years, I knew deep down inside my soul

I wanted more for my life. I felt a calling to my purpose. This wasn't the personal growth tagline that everyone said. This feeling wasn't something I could "just let go of." I couldn't keep my energy and passion locked in a cage for a minute longer. Personally, if I didn't follow my heart, I would have ended up in an asylum or a graveyard. There was no choice. I had to start taking advantage of my crisis.

I want you to know the truth about the struggles in your life. I want to show you how to see through the clutter of life and get to the facts. I want to show you how to get to the facts quickly, look within yourself for happiness, and then start to take some action to change your life. I want you to understand that if you can see through all the clutter, there is a community of people in this world who will show you the honest truth about these difficult times in our lives. These clusters of life events we call a crisis.

I have discovered that when you search for the truth, you will find it.

Remember, it can be a daunting task to find the truth. Don't expect it to be easy, but don't give up!

It is way past the time in your life to keep thinking change is easy. You must start taking advantage of your crisis! There is a positive way through your crisis. You're going to learn a ton about yourself, humanity, spirituality, and the meaning of grace through this process. It's a lot less stressful than you originally thought, too.

I want you to be in a serious crisis right now. I want you to be at a point in your life where a decision needs to be made now. A place where the universe isn't asking you to change anymore, it's demanding change, NOW. I want to help you make the right decision for your life, no matter the situation. I want to give you hope. I want to give back to you what was so freely given to me. I want to spread the infectious feeling of creativity and possibility. I want you to be alive again! You really deserve it. We all know you've been trying really hard for a really long time. It's obvious. I mean, look, you're here with me, right? Let's do this!

Okay, now get honest with yourself. Really, truly honest. Let go of your ego and pride. Let love into your heart. You need to stop paddling upstream. It's time for you to start living again and take back control of your life!

If you are honest with yourself and put in massive action, you can get the passion and drive back into your life.

I really need you to understand that people aren't just born with some magical power to be great. The people who succeed in life are the people who are being honest with themselves. They decided today that they were going to stop blaming others for their problems and take action now!

If blaming others for our problems fixed the issue, we'd stop there. However, the laws of the universe will not allow this. You must look within yourself. Look at your life review with pure honesty. Where did your problems really start? Who was really at fault? Do you think maybe if you did something a little differently, the outcome would have been positive instead?

CHAPTER 8

LACK OF PROGRESS IN YOUR LIFE: WHAT AM I DOING WRONG?!

You've been waiting too long to take action. All of us find ourselves looking at tasks in our lives, thinking that we "should" take some sort of action. For example, I should do my taxes today. I should plant a garden. I should take a cooking class. I should start taking guitar lessons. I should get a better job. I should be a better person.

I need you to understand that, right now, by replacing the word 'should' with 'must,' you will change everything in your life. As soon as you hear that oh-so-familiar word "should" in your head, you have to start changing it to the word "must!" Once all those things you should be doing become a must, your life will change automatically.

You need to start making some definitive decisions and work really hard towards them. You must make movement and change your focus entirely to be able to see what you are missing. This is the only way you can start the process of change. You must get a change of perception. This is a law of the universe.

You do not have to settle for the hypnosis of society. You do not have to compare yourself to your environment.

Being creative and having a goal will stimulate the drive for life inside of you. That feeling inside of you that something is missing? You are missing personal growth! Growth in your life is missing. We must have growth to feel alive. This is another law of the universe.

Keep in mind that, in the beginning, growth will bring pain. You have to understand that pain is normal and healthy. Pain is the only path to reward. The more pain you endure, the stronger you will be. That seems really corny, but I have come to believe in it fully. Sometimes, pushing through things, especially when it seems pointless or impossible, will bring positive growth into your life.

The goal here is to remember a time in your life when you had personal growth. Remember that experience and feel it. Remember how good it felt to be rewarded for your passionate work. That feeling of looking forward to the next day. Really visualize that moment in your life.

Connecting to a meaningful memory in your past

will bring hope. You can create a passionate life again. We always can.

I promise, through all the clutter, that personal growth is the feeling you have been searching for. You want to feel alive. That feeling will only come from growth. However, you will search elsewhere before you decide to look within yourself.

Creativity sparks passion. This is a law of the universe. I am not making this stuff up! It's empowering when you create something physical from the realm of your mind.

Maybe the opportunity to be creative isn't possible at this moment for you. When a time comes that allows you to start and become creative, take advantage of it! Even the idea of being creative will spark feelings of passion and drive. You haven't even created anything, and you've already got feelings of excitement going. Let's stay in that positive emotional state. This is the feeling you need to be chasing.

Don't give up on your primary personal goals. Continue to search for what you really want. We need this feeling of passion and drive to get creativity flowing. Passion will flow into other areas of your life. It'll make you look forward to all the things in life again. Force a smile or start dancing! With good effort, your emotions will change.

Keep that focus. Your mind is going to try and play

tricks on you. Hold true to what you know. The facts of the universe will work in your favor. Always listen to your heart. Creativity must begin. It'll blossom into a reason to live. A reason to push through anything that comes your way. Always keep the focus on positivity and movement. This will create change in every aspect of your life.

CHAPTER 9
GRATITUDE: POSITIVE FOCUS LEADS US TO NEW PERSPECTIVES

What Is gratitude?
Why should you start practicing gratitude?

In our fast-paced and often challenging world, it is easy to get caught up in the negative aspects of our lives. However, by cultivating the practice of gratitude, we can shift our focus towards the positive and unlock a world of new perspectives.

Gratitude is a powerful force that allows us to appreciate the blessings, big and small, that surround us each day. When we approach life with a grateful mind-set, we begin to notice the beauty in even the simplest things—a warm cup of coffee in the morning, a kind word from a friend, or the gentle touch of a loved one. Gratitude becomes a lens through which we view the world, allowing us to find joy and contentment in the present moment.

Beyond its ability to shift our mindset, gratitude holds the power to transform our relationships and overall well-being. When we express gratitude, whether through heartfelt words or acts of kindness, we deepen our connections with others. Gratitude strengthens bonds, fosters empathy, and creates a ripple effect of positivity.

Practicing gratitude has been scientifically linked to improved mental and physical health. It reduces stress, increases resilience, and enhances overall happiness and life overall. By accepting gratitude, we open ourselves up to an untapped source of opportunities for growth, healing, and personal transformation. I know this WILL put the drive back in your life!

Right now, I want you to stop focusing on the reasons that life is bringing you down. ONLY focus on the positive things in your life. I know it may sound silly, but once you form this habit, there will be no need to force gratitude. You will live in gratitude.

By surrounding your focus with gratitude for all things in life, you can now see a different perspective of the world. You have the power to change your reality, but it relies solely on your mental focus.

Ask the universe to take your fears and replace

them with love, and it will happen! Ask, and you will receive. A law of the universe, you will receive happiness if your focus is on love, gratitude and humility. However, asking for happiness from things outside yourself will create disappointment, a law of the universe. So, always be careful what you ask for.

CHAPTER 10

NO DAYS OFF: YOU MUST CONTINUE TO BUILD YOUR EMOTIONAL STRENGTH

Why does life seem to get more complex? Why can't I work at my job, live in my apartment, and be left alone for the rest of my life?

Remember how simple life was when you were younger? Before everything got crazy? When all you had to do was show up to school on time, and practically everything else just fell into place. Right?

Picture yourself in grade school. What were some of your biggest problems? The problems in your life, at this point in time, are probably pretty small compared to now.

Childhood problems like homework, parents, friends, bikes, parties, etc…

Overall, it's pretty easy to ignore these problems for the time being.

Don't forget, during that time of your life, those

were the biggest problems you have had! It's totally fine to be anxious, depressed or sad in those moments. It's the hardest thing you have had to do up to that point in your life!

You must not let people judge you. Everyone else around you has gone through similar problems at similar times. Everyone's at a different level with their life journey. Everyone needs a chance to see and feel experiences for the first time without being shamed for it. Let's start showing some compassion for the people around us. Everyone is facing the biggest battle of their life at this moment. Don't compare your problems with others.

Okay, let's take a step back. Now, some time has gone by, and you find yourself out of high school and living on your own. Out on the open road, for the first time, thinking of all the endless possibilities that life has in store. Finally! Right?

Sadly, no. Life events start to add up, learning "little" things on a constant basis. An entire mountain of problems that you've never faced. This is a true battle. Maybe you now have a significant other, or now you're trying to decide where in the world to go for a job or college. Possibilities seem endless during that time. You start to fear the unknown, but you find yourself still very excited.

As kids, we constantly want things to be better than

they are in actuality. Curiosity and creativity it's human nature. Children are playful and creative, but that's just what kids do, right? What does that have to do with me?

Quite literally, the problems you have today are the same style of problems you had when you were a child. It's only complex now. Life must get more complex. Don't let the word 'complex' scare you. It will overwhelm you, but we have our own meaning to this word now. This complexity is formed through all your life events. We must have endless personal growth. Without growth, we have no passion, creativity, or drive. No matter what, our lives must get more complex. Building emotional strength over time allows us to handle complex problems with grace.

So, you must continue to grow emotionally. You will be left behind if you don't. If you decide to stay behind emotionally, you will feel isolated, anxious, and depressed. You will search for emotional stability through external things around you. Resulting in substance abuse or overindulgence of some sort. This is a law of the universe. Feel your emotions to heal your emotions!

CHAPTER 11
OUR TRUE PERSONALITY: THE SELF WITHIN

I believe that an authentic personality resides within all of us. A personality slowly poking through. Penetrating this so-called 'force field' that humans have created for themselves. I call it the hypnosis of society.

The fears swirling in your mind are created by other humans just like you. Where does it say you must use the same meaning of the word as someone else? Nowhere.

What does the word anxiety mean to you? When you find out that someone close to you has been diagnosed with anxiety or depression, you can't help but get worried right away or judge them. Why? It's just an emotional state that they are in. We can all change our emotional state with focus.

Why do words make us feel so bad? As a society, we decided on specific words to create specific meanings for the objects in our environment. I mean, we had to use words eventually. We can't spend our life explaining everything around us only because we are afraid to combine the entirety of a situation or object into one word. Creating specific words for the objects around us helps us organize our lives. Words simplify the entirety of the situation. Don't let yourself get stuck on certain words unless they are full of gratitude.

Literally, these words are made up. Words that mean nothing unless you decide to attach emotions to them. It's hard not to lose mental control when you get called "depressed" or "anxious." A single word can change our entire world. These words are there to help others "understand you." It's not fair to cluster some-one's life events into one simple word. We all get depressed or anxious. You must realize it's your choice to stay in a negative state of mind. You have a choice to be happy or sad.

Your doctor has now clinically diagnosed you with a major depressive disorder with symptoms of general-ized anxiety disorder. You now need to take depression and anxiety medicines.

Now, each morning, you condition your mind with the pills, with what the doctor said, and droop your muscles. You find your breath shallow as you're hanging your head down into your lap. You've now done the complete mantra for getting into a depressive state. No!!! Stop!! Be honest with yourself; this is quite literally an incantation or mantra for an emotional state that was forced on you through societal normalities.

It's already hard to figure out who you truly are. When we listen to people living in the dead zone of life, our view of the world is skewed dramatically.

I promise that the only way to find happiness is to look within yourself. That pure personality inside of you is pushing hard to come through and present itself to you. Maybe your purpose here on earth is to find your pure personality, to find who you really are inside. Each and every one of us is so unique. If you are honest with yourself and really think about all the people in the world, every single person sees this world in a different way. Through their experiences, environment, family, friends etc. These experiences are shaping the reality we see today. Everyone is experiencing their own experiences right now, in this moment, all over the world. Your view of the world today is only your view.

This is so important. When you are able to see and hear your true personality, you must go where it needs you to go. Following what your heart says will bring you true fulfillment and happiness. You truly will feel serenity and peace.

The first most important part is to be honest with yourself, and the second most important is to have humility. Incorporating honesty with humility in every aspect of your life will remove all unwanted stresses.

We only get what we need today: the law of the universe.

When you're in a positive emotional state, fear will still reside, but this fear is healthy. It's a fear that makes you alive! What a feeling it is to be creative and willing to do the things that actually interest you. The option to make a change at any time in your life… This option is still within us! Like everything, the option can be for good or for evil.

CHAPTER 12
ALLOWING CHANGE INTO OUR LIVES: THE BATTLE BETWEEN WHAT YOU WANT AND WHAT YOU FEAR

People tend to focus on not allowing change into their lives. Most have worked hard to create a working system in their life. Works for them and them only. The thought of change starts to feel scary when you are in that place. Go back through battles to figure it all out again, just for growth? Growth is scary. We must have growth to survive, or we become rigid and dull. So, be honest with yourself; what can you do today to start your personal growth journey?

When we were kids, we didn't have the option to grow. We were forced to every day. Daily, we would be encouraged to try something new, like arts and crafts. Every single day, there was so much opportunity for growth and excitement.

The fact is this: your problems are complex now, you haven't worked on your emotional strength, and you are drinking or eating too much. Drinking and eating too much will stop emotional growth immediately.

You know that feeling right after your first drink? That moment of clarity, you can finally breathe again, people start to like you, you start to like people again, you like dancing, and you become creative with your mind. Instantly, alcohol triggers our senses, and we begin to feel alive, but these emotions are elusive.

Emotions that arise from the first drink of alcohol are equal to what you feel through working this program. It's the feeling we've all been chasing.

When you find things are not going your way, it's probably because you're not growing emotionally, or you need to grow emotionally.

People are constantly taking mental notes of what they do every day. Creating mantras for themselves unconsciously. Especially when we put in maximum effort towards a goal, only to find out it was completely wrong or a complete waste of time and money. We instantly start bashing ourselves with negative self-talk. You have got to stop doing that yourself. Find the advantage in your failures.

We always tend to think that the grass is greener on the other side. In actuality, we haven't gotten a chance to experience that part of life yet. It easily could be just as bad.

When it comes to new ideas, like moving to a new city, the possibilities are endless. Literally, you have no idea, so how could you know if it's greener on the other side? You have to feel it to know it.

In this moment of wanting change, your state of mind is future-focused on the outcome of the positive emotional state, and you're also past-focused on the negative emotional state you're in now. When you don't have control over your emotional strength, these unknowns will control your life. Learn how to strengthen your emotional strength. If you don't, you will continue to live in fear. If you're not honest with yourself, you'll either stay in the situation you've created and do nothing, or you'll bring your problems someplace else. Problems will follow you. We must feel it to heal it and then look within.

Have you ever heard that one friend say they are moving away from town to escape their problems, only to find out that their life was even worse? Most of the time, people get stuck in an endless cycle of blaming and running.

I promise you that it's 100x easier to be honest with yourself and others. Aren't we all looking to walk on the easy path of life? Wherever you can put in minimal effort, you do, right? Well, this process of becoming honest with yourself and the universe is going to be even easier. Once you become willing to be honest with yourself, you will get that feeling you've been searching for. It'll be a massive weight off your shoulders. You can sit back and breathe for a moment.

Once immersed in the program, you'll discover new emotions. You'll have a new set of eyes. You will start to see everyone around in a different light. You will come to know that everyone in this world is going through a struggle. You'll start to realize many people before you have gone through a similar crisis as you.

You'll start to see that the challenges in life were only there to promote personal growth. That then proves the point: there is, in fact, a positive in every bad situation. Now, force yourself to stay in this positive light.

You have been focusing on all the bad scenarios. Stop! Start a new habit. Remember, old habits create old results.

I get it; you don't want to look naive. You can't handle the thought of looking like a failure again, right? If you continue to focus on all the negatives of change, your life will change for the worse. Living in a negative headspace creates negative results. Crappy thoughts bring crappy results.

Instead of being in an anxious or depressed state, try this for me at least once! Force your focus on a memory that is positive or on someone who really loves you. While looking up towards the ceiling, start smiling as big as you can. Shoulders back and breathing full. Do this for 10 minutes or less; I guarantee you'll start to giggle, at least a little! This exercise is quick and produces results fast. Use it in real life; it'll help ground you, resulting in positive emotional headspace, resulting in positive results.

We have conditioned ourselves to feel anxious or depressed. Society can make a lot of money off of you when you stay in an emotional state. It's not okay to sit in those bad emotional states, though. You have to realize that you hold the power to pull yourself out of a negative emotional state. You won't escape the negativity with medication, sex, or food. It's not going to come from anything exterior. It's only going to come from within once you are truly honest with yourself.

Anytime you try something new, it will be hard, awkward, and seemingly pointless. It's in our nature to give up. Our minds scare us away from any unknown possibility. When there's no obvious danger in our environment, our animal instinct tells us to relax. There is no need to lift weights or run. This is where we need self-discipline.

How we are influenced by the people in our lives

Our parents, friends, and role models are constantly giving us advice. Why? Should I listen to them?

The answer is no. They want to shape our reality or blueprint to coincide with how they see the world. This makes them feel safe.

This is truly done to you out of love. People are just worried that they will go missing in their lives. Your loved ones don't want to see you fail. However, they tend to think interfering with your life in such a distinct way somehow they could break through to you and prevent the pain they've experienced in the past. That's all plain for me to see now.

By taking advice and listening to the people in our lives, we haven't made any decisions for ourselves yet. We have only made decisions based on what we think is right and wrong from the people around us. We think we have been making decisions for ourselves, but in actuality, the ones around us have been. We just gave a meaning to the words we heard, and that was that.

A lot of the time, the recoil of being "ourselves" will shock our loved ones. The people around us have been watching us grow, all while living up to their own life "blueprint." Lots of chaos going on in everyone's life.

So, now your loved ones notice that you have been acting differently; this gets their fears really amped up. The fear that they might lose you or be left behind. It's almost as if anything happens to you, your life will crumble. They feel they have failed you. You'll start to feel that you've failed them, too. In actuality, everyone is afraid of losing someone or something.

Most of the time, it's too complicated for the ones we love to understand us. We aren't living in each other's shoes, so I get it. They can't see a way out of their emotional fear, so maybe they can help you. They are so focused on fear and fear alone. All outcomes will reflect the emotional state you are in.

Remember, focus equals reality. What you focus on directly corresponds with the quality of your life. Fear now controls these people who care about us. They don't want to lose us.

Show someone love and patience, and you will get it in return. Every single time fear is involved, the situation becomes selfish and one-sided. It comes off as if no one really loves you, but it's the complete opposite in reality. Let go of fear. Let the universe take away your fear and everything else that's out of your control. By letting go of this fear, we can start transitioning our focus to Love. When we focus on love, we will feel love. When we are in an emotional state of love, all our decisions and outcomes will be radically different. It only takes a change in focus.

Your confidence will soar when you start to let your true personality shine. Watch out; people will mistake this energy and try to pull you back down to their level.

Why you shouldn't take a day off

As life begins to pile up problems, we continue to ignore them, thinking we deserve to have less stress and time for vacation. Life shouldn't be so intense all the time, right?!

I've heard people say stuff like, "Man, I applied for this job because I wanted to take it easy. Now, my job, which I thought was chill and would make my life easier, is adding more stress to my life. When the heck can I catch a break?"

That's what I thought, too, for a really long time. I

didn't know there was a way to change my perspective. I assumed I was the only one battling life upstream. I thought all my choices in life were wrong, stupid, naive, or downright worthless. I thought life would never change, not for me anyway. Until, one day, my problems began to be more than I could handle.

Through my research, I have come to know this; "Life isn't about taking the easy path, ignoring problems, and just having fun. I know there is a fun way to do life, but you need massive passion to accomplish that".

This is where I want to help people, to help them see that life truly is a battle for everyone, even for the richest people in the world.

That life is nothing but a mere dance between what we want and what we fear. Our fears are so strong that we even convince ourselves of the lies.

Life is about excitement, drive, passion, and hope. Let me show you how to master the building blocks to achieve constant motivation and positivity throughout every single day. The possibilities are endless.

CHAPTER 13
THE SECRET TO A POSITIVE EMOTIONAL STATE

Finally, I present to you the building blocks of your divine path.

You must write these steps down on a piece of paper and read them as soon as you wake up every morning. No exceptions.

1. Get out of bed right away, no matter what.
2. Start moving your body right away. Start with stretching your muscles. By moving your body first thing in the morning, your metabolism is now activated. If you don't jump-start your metabolism in the morning, you will continue to gain fat and lose muscle, especially with age.
3. Begin to Focus on Gratitude. Start to visualize all the people who unconditionally

love you. Close your eyes and create a network of love through all these people. Start picturing a time in your life when the sensations around you created a certain memory and feeling, producing tranquility within you. You are now in a positive emotional state.

4. Start to focus on your primary goal. This MUST happen to jump-start creativity and good emotion. DO NOT FOCUS ON FEAR (Anxiety, depression, and unknowns)

5. Manage your focus solely on your goal. You MUST ignore bad memories from the past. Deny your mind to think negative. Complete focus.

6. Don't think about what you "have" to do. Once you start visualizing that your primary goal is something that "has to be done," ALL creativity, passion, drive, and purpose will disappear.

7. Start to change your perspective on what you can create today. Focus on the positive aspects of every situation. Getting into the right state of mind takes movement and complete focus. Change the way you use your body, and it will change the way you feel.

8. Now, let's start an incantation. You must say this OUTLOUD, "Every day, in every way, I am getting stronger and stronger." Repeat this mantra for 15 to 45 minutes. Your body will start vibrating with power.

9. Time to take a moment and celebrate. Pushing yourself that hard is unique and takes impeccable strength! You're the man, and you're the one who's not afraid of change!! You've accomplished a goal!!

10. Now, you MUST keep the momentum.

These steps changed my life when I was in a crisis. I know they will do the same for you; trust me, this works. Give these steps an honest try, and give it your all. These things are meant to be enjoyed, so get outside and be creative with how you exercise. It doesn't have to be boring.

Start Taking Advantage of Your Crisis today with these steps!

CHAPTER 14
CHAKRAS: INTRODUCTION TO HOW CHAKRAS INFLUENCE OUR EMOTIONS, HEALTH, AND OVERALL WELL-BEING

I found it crucial to include a basic introduction to chakras. In modern society, particularly in the US, the term 'chakra' often carries negative connotations. It is frequently disregarded without much thought, almost as if it is associated with mystical practices. Let's challenge the stereotypes surrounding chakras and focus on healing in alignment with the natural order of the universe.

The human body consists of numerous energy channels called 'nadis,' which form energy vortexes known as chakras. These chakras, located along the spine in 7 different positions, are associated with specific body parts and emotions. When a chakra is blocked, it disrupts the flow of energy and affects the related aspects of life. Balancing and aligning the chakras through visualization and meditation will directly bring serenity and harmony to one's well-being.

Muladhara - Root Chakra

In life, we must start with a building block. We have to start somewhere. Muladhara is our root chakra. This chakra is associated with the color red.

The root chakra connects you to this earth. Helping you stay grounded in mother nature. Its role is to give us the basics we need to survive. When the root chakra is balanced, we feel secure in all aspects of life, including financial and emotional situations. The way to balance your root chakra is to get out of the house and into the elements. Nature is full of medicine. Relax your mind, and you'll find it.

Svadishthana - Sacral Chakra

Just below the belly button lies the sacral chakra. Admitting an orange color, this haven of pleasurable activities is the creative life force that grants us the feeling of being alive. This chakra, Svadishthana, involves our sexual emotions. It is easy for humans to focus on that. Don't. A common misconception. The sacral chakra offers more. It must include an array of things that make YOU happy... which, for a lot of us, might be having sex with our partner! Sex is a part of life. Sex involves higher frequencies of emotion that

are hard to comprehend. Just do what feels humane.

Manipura - Solar Plexus

The Manipura chakra is all about personal growth. This chakra shines yellow in color. This is the location at which we have the power to create our self-confidence, authenticity and identity. This chakra is also known as the solar plexus.

When you say, "I have a 'gut' feeling," it relates back to the chakra, solar plexus.

This chakra offers the power of knowledge to really know what feels right. This voice is part of our divine path.

When the Manipura chakra is balanced, you will feel connected to your personal wisdom and truth. Allowing you to be honest with yourself in every situation.

I like to call it the warrior chakra. It will produce feelings of confidence and strength. Just be sure and direct this energy in a humane way. Your 'gut' will let you know!

Anahata Chakra - Heart Chakra

The Anahata chakra is where we connect with love.

It activates the sense of feeling loved, knowing we are worthy of love and sending out love. This chakra shines a green color. Located smack in the middle of your chest, this is the heart chakra.

Compassion towards yourself and others is vital for life. When this chakra is well taken care of, you'll be able to accept and receive love equally, even in tricky situations.

People tend to give a lot more love to others than we give to ourselves. This will knock your heart chakra out of balance.

There are very simple ways to make sure this chakra stays in balance. You must do one thing each day that is fully for you. It could be a relaxing bath, a walk around your favorite park, or maybe an evening watching your favorite film. My personal favorite is a self-love meditation. Poke around with multiple guided meditations until you find one or more that feels right for you.

Vishudda - Throat Chakra

Shining a blue color, the Vishudda is about communication. This is the throat chakra. Make sure you use this with love, kindness and honesty. Knowing which words to use in certain situations is a sign of a balanced throat chakra, but as with all of the chakras, it can easily be put out of balance.

Something you can do to help this is to always think before you speak. Take a moment to assess the situation and ask yourself if what you're about to say is kind and necessary. However, most of all, remember to always speak with honesty!

Anja Chakra - Third Eye Chakra

My personal favorite chakra, coming in at number 6 and shining an indigo color, is the Anja chakra. Placed right between your eyes, people today call it the third eye chakra. This is where wisdom, intuition, and psychic energy reside.

A lot of us are disconnected from our Anja chakra. As a society, we are used to not feeling spiritual experiences. So, why would we start? Seems fake to us til we actually feel it. We must open our minds in order to even entertain the energetic possibilities that are available to us.

Have fun and explore guided meditations that focus on the Anja chakra. It takes time to be patient and open-minded. You'll discover powers only told in stories.

Sahasrara - Crown Chakra

Last but not least, located at the crown of our craniums and brightly shining, the color violet/white, is the Sahasrara chakra.

Also known as the crown chakra, this is where everything comes together in unity. Connecting our inner world with the entire universe around us. I like saying this chakra is the 'universal energy, whereas everything is one.'

Having a balanced crown chakra will lead you to enlightenment. In the modern world, this is very taboo.

However, that doesn't mean you can't start practicing today.

To energize the crown chakra, work is needed on the lower six chakras first. Once they are aligned, you'll be able to access the universal connection to your divine path. Allowing you to see clearly what you are meant to do while on Earth.

Understanding how chakras work offers a transformative journey toward self-discovery and well-being. It's important to cultivate awareness and balance within our energy centers. Granting your true potential enhances your physical, mental, and emotional health. In addition, knowledge of chakras will align us with a harmonious and fulfilling existence. Embrace the power of chakras, find your inner self, and embark on a lifelong path of self-care and spiritual growth. May this beginner's guide to chakras open your mind to new possibilities. Illuminate this empowering and radiant energy in every aspect of your life!

CHAPTER 15

FROM CRISIS TO OPPORTUNITY: EMBRACING GROWTH AND SELF-DISCIPLINE

We must get a better understanding of human instincts. We must get a better understanding of our hearts.

We must learn how to listen to the voice within us. It is telling us what is right and wrong for the purpose of all humanity. This is where we can come to a conclusion on this fact: there are two voices speaking to us. It's not as simple as good and evil. It's even more simple. What our body is telling us is required for physical survival. What our heart is telling us is for the divine path.

What exactly is human instinct? Human instinct is intact for the survival of our physical body. Think way way way back in time. A time when humans were forced to be hunters and gatherers. They had to withstand the natural elements day in and day out. No matter what was around them, there was always a chance they'd have to face a fierce predator in the wild.

Remember, we have these fear responses so we can escape quickly. In these situations, we don't have time to think. Our unconscious mind makes decisions for us. This instinct also controls our sexual desires subconsciously. Our main human instincts are self-preservation (life and death), sexual desires (the human race must live on), and our social status (how we fit in with everyone).

We have no control over our human instincts, but we do have control over our divine path.

When we don't listen to our hearts, we get stuck in a state of survival. The only way to get out of the state of survival is through honestly listening to your heart over and over. Make it a habit. Habits form who you are. We must only live in a state of divine power. Start listening to your "gut" feeling more. Your divine path is humane and right; it will not guide you wrong.

Sometimes, situations in life seem so unfair, but if you can stop worrying for just a little while, then can you listen to your heart (gut feeling)?

Your life has a much higher meaning than you think. You must trust the process of the divine path and listen to your gut feeling (heart) with honesty, no matter what may arise in your life. Everything else will fall into place perfectly. You will at last know the meaning of the word serenity. You will see who you truly are. You will feel balanced and whole.

The journey on the divine path is endless. Once you understand this spiritual feeling, the word "endless" will excite you. We must have something to look forward to!

I know this to be the secret to life, at least for me. The divine path is extremely fulfilling, and it drives me forward every day.

Learn about the psychology of human instinct. Reflect on the concept of 'following your heart.' Consider whether you prefer living in a state of constant stress or in a state of peace. Instead of complaining, seize the opportunity presented by your current challenges!!

Made in the USA
Columbia, SC
28 June 2024